Science Discoveries

ALEXANDER GRAHAM

BELL

and the Telephone

Steve Parker

Chelsea House Publishers
New York • Philadelphia

This edition © Chelsea House Publishers 1995

First published in Great Britain in 1994
by Belitha Press Limited

Copyright © Belitha Press Limited 1994

Text © Steve Parker 1994

Illustrations/photographs copyright © in this
format by Belitha Press Limited 1994

1 3 5 7 9 8 6 4 2

ISBN 0-7910-3004-0
Printed in China for Imago

Photographic credits:
AT&T 27
AT&T Archives 7 top, 13 top left and bottom, 14
inset.
Bridgeman Art Library 6 bottom Guildhall Art
Gallery, London, 9 center Christie's London.
Mary Evans Picture Library 7 bottom, 17 bottom
left, 18 top, 22 top, 23 bottom left, 25 bottom, 29.
Michael Holford 10 top (both), 15 bottom left.
Hulton Deutsch Collection 5 bottom left, 16 top,
24 bottom.
Image Select 10 bottom, 14, 15 bottom right, 21
bottom.
Mansell Collection 8 bottom, 9 bottom, 24 top.
Science Museum, London 4 top, 5 top and bottom
right, 7 center, 12, 13 top right, 17 top and bottom
right, 18 bottom, 22 bottom, 23 top and bottom
right.
Science Photo Library title page and 25 top Library
of Congress, 4 bottom Alfred Pasieka, 15 top, 16
bottom, 20 top and 21 top J-L Charmet, 26 top
David Parker, 26 bottom Will and Deni McIntyre.

Cover images provided by Hulton Deutsch
Collection, Ann Ronan Picture Library, The
Science Museum, Mary Evans Picture Library

Illustrations by Tony Smith
Diagrams by Peter Bull

Editor: Struan Reid
Design: Cooper Wilson Limited
Picture research: Juliet Duff
Specialist adviser: Marina Benjamin

Contents

Even in his later years, "Father of the telephone" Alexander Graham Bell was a tireless experimenter and inventor.

Telephone technology advances ever faster, with fax machines and hand-sized mobile phones linked by radio to the network.

Introduction

The telephone is a vital part of our daily life. It is essential for business, transport, travel, and many communications of all kinds. It is often difficult to imagine life without it. Yet only 120 years ago the telephone did not exist.

A number of different people contributed to the invention of the telephone. The most important was Alexander Graham Bell. From about 1872, he spent many years developing his dream – the "speaking telegraph."

At the time, many exciting new developments were taking place in the world of electricity. Inventors were working on all kinds of electrical devices, from light bulbs to motors, and various types of telephones. Bell's was recognized as the first fully-working version. Just as he hoped, his invention brought him fame, fortune, and success, and truly changed the world.

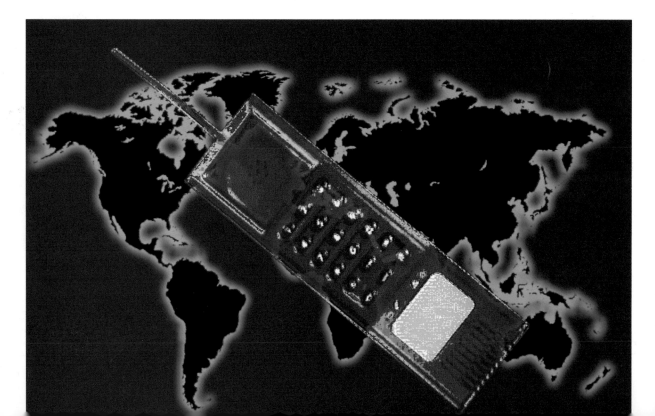

Chapter One
The Early Years

Alexander Bell was born on March 3, 1847, in the city of Edinburgh, Scotland. His father, Alexander Melville Bell, was a professor at Edinburgh University. His mother, Eliza, looked after Alexander and his two brothers, Melville and Edward.

Alexander senior was professor of elocution and the art of speech. This meant he was an expert in the processes and skills of speech. He taught people how to talk clearly and distinctly.

Hearing and Speech

Alexander senior was also interested in helping people with hearing difficulties. Some of these, especially children, developed speech problems because they could not hear other people or themselves. So they did not know how clear speech should sound, or how to produce it.

Eliza Bell herself had considerable hearing problems, though she was still able to teach her sons for a period of time. Alexander junior, called Aleck in his family, was eager to read and learn.

In the 19th century, people with poor hearing used devices such as speaking funnels and these ear trumpets.

Eliza Bell taught her sons for a period of time, despite her hearing difficulties.

Edinburgh University, where Alexander Graham Bell's father taught.

5

Why Alexander "Graham" Bell?

At the age of 11, Alexander asserted his independence from his father by altering his name. A friend called Alexander Graham visited the Bell family. From this time, young Alexander called himself Alexander Graham Bell.

An Average Pupil

The mid-19th century was a time of booming industry in Britain. Cities like Edinburgh were smoky and noisy from the factories and machinery. The Bell family did not enjoy the best of health, so their father bought a second house in the Scottish countryside. Alexander loved the flowers and animals, and enjoyed his breaks away from the city.

At the age of 11, Alexander was sent to the Royal Edinburgh High School. But he disliked the school routine and the strict lessons in subjects such as Greek and Latin. He left only two years later with no proper qualifications.

Down to London

The Bell family was not pleased with young Alexander's lack of school success. So he was sent to London to stay with his grandfather, who was a speech expert.

Alexander enjoyed the independence of London. He got along well with his grandfather and improved in his studies. He also learned much about the human voice box (**larynx**) and speech production.

London in the 19th century was smoky, noisy, and crowded. Yet Aleck enjoyed his time with his grandfather. He learned many speeches from the plays of William Shakespeare.

The Art of Speech

As Alexander Graham Bell was growing up, there were no **microphones**, loudspeakers, or public address systems. Speakers and lecturers aimed to talk loudly and clearly, but without strain or shouting.

People entertained each other using musical instruments and their own voices, with singing, poetry, and acting, so the ability to speak well was important in daily life. Lessons in elocution, the art of clear speaking, were very popular.

Scientist Michael Faraday speaks at the Royal Institution, 1855.

Alexander poses for his photograph in front of some "outdoor" scenery. This was in his student years, when he was about 16 or 17 years old.

A Start in Teaching

Alexander applied for a post as a teacher of elocution and music at Weston House Academy in Elgin, Scotland. He got the job, even though he was only 16 years old and younger than some of his pupils!

After a year in Elgin, Alexander returned to Edinburgh University to study Latin and Greek. He taught again in Elgin and then in Bath, England. During this time he studied how the voice worked, feeling his own neck for the fast to-and-fro movements, or vibrations. He read about the **acoustic** (sound) experiments of the German scientist Hermann von Helmholtz. He thought that speech might be able to be transmitted by "waves" of electricity along a wire.

Hermann von Helmholtz (1821-1894) studied electricity and magnetism. Bell studied his work on acoustics.

7

Visible Speech

Alexander Bell senior spent about 15 years devising a system of symbols which he called Visible Speech. These symbols worked like an alphabet, but for sounds instead of letters. Each set of symbols showed the position of the mouth, tongue, lips, and throat to make the sound. In this way, sounds could be written down, rather than letters.

A Time in London

For many years, Alexander Bell senior had been working on his system of Visible Speech (see sidebar). In 1866 he and his family moved to London, and the next year Alexander junior joined them. He started teaching his father's system to children with hearing and speech problems. He carried on his voice and electrical experiments, and also found himself a girlfriend.

A Fresh Start

Ill health continued to affect the Bells. In 1867, Alexander's younger brother Edward became ill and died. In 1868, Alexander senior went on a tour of North America. He thought that Visible Speech might be more accepted there than it had been in London, and also that the climate might be healthier for his sickly family. In 1870 he decided to move there when his oldest son, Melville, also died.

At first, Alexander junior wanted to stay in England with his teaching job, studies and his girlfriend. But, as the last surviving son, he decided to leave with his parents for a new life in Canada in July 1870. He was 23 years old.

Alexander began taking courses at London University, but he had to leave when he moved to Canada.

Chapter Two
Helping Hands

The Bell family arrived in Quebec, Canada, in August 1870. The next year, young Alexander went to Boston, Massachusetts. A woman named Sarah Fuller had started a school there for children with hearing and speech difficulties, using Visible Speech. Bell got a job as a teacher at the school.

Professor Bell hoped that plenty of fresh air and an outdoor lifestyle in Canada would improve his health and his family's.

Sound and Vibrations

Bell soon became established in Boston as a successful teacher. He showed his pupils how speech sounds were produced by the very fast to-and-fro movements, or vibrations, of the vocal cords in the voice box. He demonstrated how these vibrations were altered by the positions of the lips, teeth and tongue.

Bell encouraged his pupils to place their fingertips gently on his neck, jaw, cheeks, mouth, and lips, and feel the vibrations as he spoke. Then they would feel their own necks and mouths, and try to make sounds which produced the same feelings.

The staff and pupils of Boston School for the Deaf, 1871. Sarah Fuller, who founded the school, is second from the left in the second row from the back. Dark-bearded Alexander Graham Bell is at top right.

The Telegraph

As Bell grew up in Scotland, there was already a method of sending long-distance messages in the blink of an eye. It was the **telegraph**, which carried electrical signals along wires. But these were on/off codes, not the varied pattern of signals that represented sounds, which was Bell's aim.

• In 1837 Englishmen William Cooke and Charles Wheatstone made the first working telegraph. It was used to back up visual signals on the railways. They sent pulses of electricity along a wire which made a needle at the other end swing to-and-fro on a dial. The dial was marked with the alphabet so that the needle swings spelled out letters and words.

• Around the same time, American Samuel Morse developed the Morse code system of dots and dashes for letters and numbers. In 1844 he sent long-distance messages over 37 miles. The most famous Morse message is the emergency signal SOS (three dots followed by three dashes followed by three dots).

The swinging needle display of the Cooke and Wheatstone telegraph, 1844, as used at Paddington Railway Station.

The Morse sender-receiver of about 1850, which inked dots and dashes onto a paper tape.

Telegraph offices soon opened in cities and towns. This is the office of the London-Paris telegraph link, 1852.

Encouragement not Punishment

Bell tried to teach using patience and encouragement, rather than traditional strictness and punishment. He helped children who were expected never to speak. The work brought him great pleasure and many grateful pupils.

Bell continued to teach by day and experiment on the telegraph in the evening. One problem with the telegraph was that it could send only one message at a time in each direction (the duplex system). Lines were always busy and people waited in line to send messages. Bell believed that if several different signals could be sent over the same wire at the same time, this invention would earn a fortune.

Bell thought that separate messages could be sent by making their electricity "vibrate" at different rates. But the work was exhausting, and he did not fully understand the electrical side of it.

When teaching deaf people to speak, Bell placed their fingertips on his own throat and mouth, and spoke certain words. The students felt the types of vibrations, then touched their own necks and mouths, and tried to copy the pattern of vibrations.

11

Metal reed

Make-and-break electrical switch

The Harmonic Telegraph

Bell's idea for a multi-message telegraph depended on two processes — harmonic resonance and electro**magnetism**.

To show resonance, put two guitars near each other, and pluck a string on one. The string sends out sound waves of a certain **frequency** (the number of waves per second). The sound waves hit the strings on the other guitar. The same string there, and only this string, begins to vibrate "in sympathy." This is called resonance.

When an **electric current** passes through a wire, it creates a magnetic field around the wire. If an iron rod is placed in the center of a coil of wire and the electricity is turned on, the rod becomes magnetic. This is called an electro-magnet.

Bell's idea was to send messages along a wire as on/off codes, from different-sized vibrating metal strips called reeds. Each sending reed acted as a very fast on/off switch that produced an electrical signal which varied at the same speed as its own vibrations.

At the other end of the wire, the electrical signals passed through several electromagnets. Near each was a receiving reed, "tuned" to its equivalent sending reed. The receiving reed would be attracted by the electromagnet and vibrate, but only in resonance to signals from its sending reed.

In this way, several sets of signals, each with a different frequency, could be sent along one wire at the same time. Each receiving reed would respond when its sending partner was vibrated.

Electromagnet

Clamp

Wire terminals

Wooden base

Part of Bell's harmonic telegraph, showing a sender and receiver. Each has a tuned reed — the dark, flat, horizontal metal plate. Each reed has one end clamped and the other end free to vibrate above the electromagnet (coil of wire).

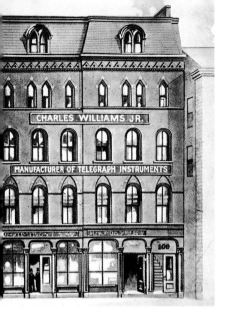

Williams', the Boston shop where Bell bought most of his electrical supplies. He met Watson here, and carried out his experiments in the attic.

Back to Boston

In Boston, Bell became professor of vocal **physiology** at the university there. He lived with the wealthy Thomas Sanders and his family.

The next year, a 15-year-old girl, Mabel Hubbard, became one of Bell's occasional pupils. She had lost her hearing at the age of four or five, as a result of **scarlet fever**. Her father was a rich Boston businessman and lawyer named Gardiner Hubbard. Bell fell in love with Mabel, and after a time, she fell in love with him. They would become engaged in 1875 and marry two years later.

Money and Backing

Bell told Hubbard and Sanders about his ideas for the multitelegraph and telephone. But this was a race for success and fortune since there were other inventors working on the same ideas.

Hubbard and Sanders agreed to provide money to support Bell in his work. They also agreed to rent a workshop for Bell, and hire a part-time assistant called Thomas Watson.

A Trustworthy Assistant

Thomas Watson worked at Williams', a Boston electrical shop. At first Bell was unsure of his new assistant, but the two soon got along well and were hard at work in the invention race. Watson was loyal and enthusiastic, and had electrical skills that made up for the gaps in Bell's knowledge.

Thomas Watson (1854-1934) was Bell's hardworking assistant for over five years. He then took up farming and eventually became a successful shipbuilder.

Mabel Hubbard, about age 18. She learned to lip-read and speak clearly, helped by her mother, her governess, and Bell.

13

A rebuilt version of Bell's laboratory in the attic of Williams' shop (see the window from the outside on page 13).

A drawing of Bell applying for his telephone patent on February 14, 1876. In fact, Hubbard went to Washington to make the application.

Chapter Three

Toward the Telephone

Bell was well aware of the progress being made by rival inventor Elisha Gray. As it turned out, the two men applied for official approval and patents for their telephones within a few hours of each other (see page 17). Arguments would continue for years about who invented the telephone first.

A Stuck Reed

In 1875, Bell and Watson worked to improve the harmonic telegraph (see page 12). On June 2, Bell was in the transmitter room with three sending reeds. A single wire led to a nearby room with Watson and the three receiving reeds.

One of the receiving reeds got stuck. As Watson tried to get it free, Bell was in the other room watching the sending reeds – and one of them vibrated enough to make a sound. It was sound being turned into electricity and back to sound again, by the principle of electromagnetic induction (see page 15).

Famous American scientist Joseph Henry (1797-1878) encouraged Bell. He had developed electromagnets, electric motors and the relay switch for long-distance telegraphy.

A Mixture of Sounds

Bell saw that here was the basic way to make a "speaking telegraph." He thought back to a device that he had sketched in the summer of 1874, while on vacation with his parents in Ontario. It was like a multiple telegraph, but in the shape of a harp, with many different-length reeds (metal strips) for the "strings."

Bell knew that sounds such as speech and music consist of a mixture of sound waves of various frequencies and strengths. By resonance, each of the reeds would pick up and vibrate to its own particular frequency of sound. The reeds would make the electrical signals that went along a wire to a similar harp-shaped reed-receiver. This then reversed the process to remake the original pattern of sounds.

Electromagnetic Induction

Induction is the opposite of the electromagnetic effect. If a wire is put near a magnet, electricity will be generated, or "induced," and will flow through the wire. The **magnetic field** must be moving or varying in strength in relation to the wire, or no electricity flows.

In 1873, Bell had imagined a metal strip, like a reed, that was also a magnet. It vibrated at a certain speed near a coil of wire, and induced an electrical signal in the wire that varied at the same speed. However, Bell believed the electricity would be very weak, and so useless. He did not bother to test the idea. The stuck reed of 1875 showed that he had been wrong.

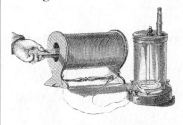

Moving a magnet inside an induction coil to make electricity.

Bell read about pioneers of electricity such as Michael Faraday (1791-1867, see also page 7). Faraday and Henry discovered electromagnetic induction in the 1830s.

15

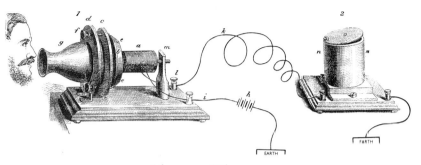

*A working illustration of one of Bell's experimental telephones. The lines at "b" represent the **battery** powering the device.*

The Importance of Patents

A patent is a description of an invention which is registered and kept by the authorities, to show who thought of it first. For a set period of time afterward, only the inventor can make, use or sell the invention. The inventor can also give permission to others to do so or sell the patent to others. Patents are very important if an invention becomes successful, because the person who owns the patent earns the money.

Almost There

To improve on the idea of multiple reed receivers and transmitters, Bell took an idea from his knowledge of speech, hearing and anatomy. The human ear contains a thin, tightly-stretched **membrane** called an eardrum. This responds as it is hit by sound waves. It vibrates in a complicated way to many frequencies, not in the simple way a strip-shaped reed does to a single frequency.

Bell thought that perhaps a thin, flexible skin or **parchment** sheet, called a diaphragm, could act as a mechanical eardrum. An electromagnet attached to the diaphragm would convert the pattern of its vibrations, produced by sound waves, into a similar pattern of electrical signals in the wire. At the other end of the wire, a similar device would turn the electrical signals back to sounds (see page 20).

By June 1875, Bell and Watson showed that the principle could work. They were very close to a real working telephone, but the sounds it produced were fuzzy and unclear, and no words could be made out.

Another early telephone, based on a flexible membrane that looks like a drum skin at the bottom. It vibrates in response to sounds, and the magnet attached to it induces electrical signals in the coil of wire above.

Chapter Four
The First Telephones

On February 14, 1876, Gardiner Hubbard took Bell's patent for the telephone to the U.S. Patent Office. Just a few hours later the same day, Elisha Gray also applied for a patent for a telephone.

Just in time

Bell's patent application was accepted on March 3, 1876 (his 29th birthday) as U.S. patent number 174,465. It was one of the most valuable patents in history. Later, Gray and Bell became involved in a long **legal** battle over who was first.

A replica of Bell's "centennial" telephone transmitter of 1876. It is similar to the version illustrated opposite.

Strictly, the machine Bell described in the patent could not send the clear sounds of a voice by electricity along a wire. Gray's version of the telephone was still an idea at the time, since he had not built it. But his design would have worked much better. Finally the U.S. Supreme Court ruled that Bell was the official inventor of the telephone.

Bell, photographed in 1876, the year the telephone came into being.

A new pastime — chatting to friends on the telephone. This version has a separate mouthpiece and earpiece.

Thomas Edison (1847-1931) was the greatest inventor of his day. He wanted to make machines and devices that would make life easier and more comfortable for the average person, as well as earn him money!

Bell's Great Rivals

American scientist and inventor Elisha Gray (1835-1901) worked on many electrical devices. In 1867 he devised a self-adjusting relay switch for the telegraph: like Bell he wanted to develop a multiple telegraph. In 1888 he came up with the telautograph, a telegraph-based machine that could transmit patterns of dots and lines on paper — a very early attempt at the **facsimile** (fax) machine.

American inventor and businessman Thomas Edison (1847-1931) became rich and world-famous. His achievements included improving the telegraph and inventing the light bulb, the **phonograph** (a type of gramophone), and early movie equipment. In 1882 Edison set up the world's first electricity **power station** and supply network to offices, shops, and houses in New York.

Edison heard about Bell's telephone in 1875, and within a year he had invented his own version. In fact Edison's carbon-button design is the one used in telephones today.

A wall-mounted Edison telephone, from about 1880. In his carbon microphone, sound waves compressed the carbon granules in a small container or button. This altered the pattern of electricity passing through them.

A Call for Help

The next major development in Bell's telephone came on March 10, 1876, only days after his patent was issued. Bell sat with a test transmitter in one room. Wires connected it to the receiver in the next room, where Watson was working. The story goes that Bell spilt some dangerous acid chemicals. Urgently he shouted into the transmitter: "Mr. Watson, come here, I want to see you!" Watson came through and said that he had heard Bell's voice and made out the words. The first message spoken over the telephone was a call for help!

Over the following weeks Bell and Watson made new designs and adjustments to improve the quality of the sound. For us today, Bell's early telephones would sound crackly, muffled and unclear. But at the time, the idea of hearing voices coming from a machine, rather than a person, seemed like a miracle.

Watson comes to help Bell after hearing his call for assistance over the telephone. In great excitement they took turns to speak and read from books. Bell sang the British national anthem. He wrote: "The effect was loud but indistinct and muffled.... Finally the sentence 'Mr. Bell, do you understand what I say?' came quite clear and intelligibly."

One of Bell's combined transmitter-receiver telephones, from 1877, where the single unit was both mouthpiece and earpiece.

Could it Be Useful?

At first, spoken messages could go only one way along the wire: from transmitter to receiver. The listener had to send messages back by telegraph. Bell soon put a transmitter and receiver together at each end, and also designed a dual-purpose transmitter-receiver, for two-way conversations.

However, would the telephone ever be useful? Perhaps it might stay a scientific toy or **novelty**, as Hubbard once thought. Bell needed to show it to people, so they could see and hear it working and understand its possibilities. Only in this way could he get support and money for setting up huge telephone **networks**, to rival and replace the telegraph.

Bell needed to convince people that the telephone would change their lives.

The Early Telephone

In this age of mobile phones smaller than a hand, Bell's first versions of the telephone look large and clumsy. But telephones soon became smaller, lighter, and more reliable, and transmitted clearer, louder sounds. Here is how an early model worked.

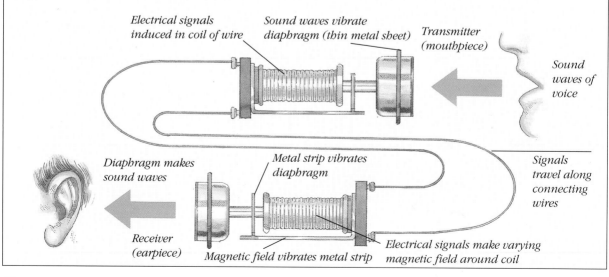

Electrical signals induced in coil of wire

Sound waves vibrate diaphragm (thin metal sheet)

Transmitter (mouthpiece)

Sound waves of voice

Signals travel along connecting wires

Diaphragm makes sound waves

Metal strip vibrates diaphragm

Receiver (earpiece)

Magnetic field vibrates metal strip

Electrical signals make varying magnetic field around coil

Chapter Five

From Novel Toy to Vital Tool

At the great 1876 Centenary Exhibition in Philadelphia, Bell saw an opportunity for his telephone to be noticed. Many scientists and businesspeople would be visiting the exhibition, as well as many other prominent people.

One important visitor to the exhibition was Emperor Pedro II of Brazil. His enthusiasm for the **demonstration** of Bell's telephone made the headlines in the next day's newspapers.

Over Long Distances

The next stage was to see if the telephone could work over long distances. A landmark came when Bell gave a lecture about the telephone in Salem, Massachusetts. He showed that he could talk to Watson, who was at the other end in Boston, nearly 19 miles away.

Although there was great interest in the new device, the giant telegraph companies feared competition from the telephone and encouraged false **rumors** about its bad effects.

Bell demonstrated his telephone to many influential people, including Scottish scientist William Thomson, later Lord Kelvin. Thomson became Bell's main supporter in Britain.

Doubts and Worries

At first, people were suspicious of telephones. This was a time when few people had first-hand experience of electrical machines, even telegraphs. There were fears that other people could also listen in on the telephone conversations, or that the sounds from telephones could make you deaf or crazy.

Bell describes his telephone to the audience in Salem on February 12, 1877. He amazed them by talking to Watson, far away in Boston. Many people suspected it was a hoax.

21

Queen Victoria was treated to a demonstration of the telephone at her Isle of Wight home and called it "most extraordinary."

The Bell Telephone Company

As people found out more about the telephone, they understood that the rumors were untrue. On July 9, 1877, Bell, Watson, Gardiner Hubbard, and Thomas Sanders formed the Bell Telephone Company. Bell married Mabel Hubbard on July 11, 1877, two days after setting up his company.

Bell had turned the telephone from a dream into reality. But this relatively simple device needed manufacturing, marketing, and selling. He left most of this work to Hubbard and the others. He once said: "Financial dealings are distasteful to me and not at all in my line."

A New Generation

On their honeymoon in Britain, the Bells traveled to many of the places Alexander had known in his youth. Soon Mabel was expecting a baby, so they delayed their return by a year.

It was not a complete rest. The telephone was becoming famous. Bell was asked to give many lectures and demonstrations, including one to Queen Victoria. Around this time, Elisha Gray and several others fought Bell's patents in the law courts. Bell wrote to a friend: "The more fame a man gets for an invention, the more does he become a target for the world to shoot at."

On May 8, 1879, Mabel had a baby, who they named Elsie. In October, the Bells and their new daughter returned to Canada to spend time with Alexander's parents.

The Bell Osborne model of the telephone, dated 1878, in honor of Queen Victoria. (Her Isle of Wight home was called Osborne House.)

Chapter Six
Wires Across the World

To begin with, wires connected each telephone or "speaking telegraph" with every other. The growing number of users produced a huge web of wires. So telephone exchanges were developed. All local phones were connected to it by their own wires. A test exchange was built in Boston, now known as the Home of the Telephone, in 1877.

Sick of the Telephone

Bell had decided that he was sick of the telephone, and told his wife so. By 1880, he had left the world of telephones and patent battles. He resigned from the Bell Telephone Company, although the money from his invention made him a wealthy man for the rest of his life. The Bells had another daughter, Marian.

Bell was only 33 years old, and he had achieved his main ambitions. He had invented a device that was changing people's lives, and he was rich and world-famous. He decided that he wanted to carry on inventing, and he did this for the next 40 years.

Telephone Design

Many different designs for the telephone sprang up in the late 19th century. To be successful, a telephone had to be elegant to look at. Inside, the working parts were all much the same.

Candlestick-on-holder, 1901

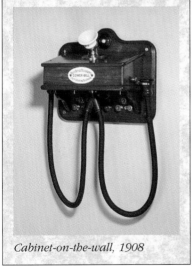

Cabinet-on-the-wall, 1908

The Paris telephone exchange, 1904. Exchanges provided plenty of work, particularly for women.

23

Bell sits for a studio portrait in the late 1880s. His place in history was assured, and he had moved on to other inventions.

More Inventions

The Bell family moved to Washington, D.C. In 1880 he was awarded the Volta Prize and 50,000 francs by France. He used this money to set up the Volta Laboratory in Washington. It was named after Alessandro Volta, who invented the battery (electrical **cell**) in 1800. Bell wanted it to become an "inventions factory" like that of Thomas Edison.

From 1880 Bell worked on an idea he called the photophone. This used light instead of electricity to carry a pattern of signals representing sounds. (Modern optical-fiber phone lines do this, see page 26.) He also improved Edison's phonograph. In 1882 Bell became a U.S. citizen.

The Later Years

Bell still worked and **campaigned** for people with speech and hearing problems. In 1886 he bought a summer home at Baddeck Bay on the remote Cape Breton Island off Nova Scotia, Canada. It reminded him of his boyhood in the Scottish countryside. There he built a **laboratory** so he could work even while he was on vacation.

In 1892, Alexander Graham Bell spoke on the opening of the telephone link between New York and Chicago. Phone wires were being laid to all parts of the U.S. and Canada, and across many countries in Europe.

Bell was a member of the Aerial Experimental Association, which produced this Silver Dart *airplane in 1909, along with hydrofoil boats.*

Planes and Boats

Bell continued to experiment and invent. Among his numerous projects, he designed, built, and flew many different kites. In 1908, his team built a plane that won an aviation **trophy**. In 1908, he also turned to water and developed a hydrofoil, a boat with "skis" that skims over the surface.

Not on the Phone

Bell became a burly, white-haired father figure to the world of science and communication. He received awards and prizes from many organizations and countries.

In 1922, at the age of 75, Bell suddenly fell ill at Cape Breton. He died peacefully on August 2, with Mabel beside him. To the end of his life, Bell refused to have a telephone in his workroom. He said that he did not want it to interrupt him.

Alexander Graham Bell was buried at his Cape Breton home of Beinn Bhreagh on August 4, 1922. At the same time, all telephones in the United States went quiet for one minute in his honor.

Telephone Landmarks

1878 First telephone exchanges open.

1886-87 Thomas Edison invents the carbon-button mouthpiece that would eventually take over from Bell's version.

1887 There are more than 1,000 exchanges and 150,000 telephones in the U.S., 26,000 telephones in Britain, 9,000 in France, and 22,000 in Germany.

1889 Undertaker Almon Strowger has the idea for the automatic exchange, so callers can dial direct, without operators.

1892 The first direct-connection exchange opens in La Porte, Indiana; Bell makes the first long-distance call between New York and Chicago.

1915 Bell in New York and Watson in San Francisco make the first call right across the United States.

One of Bell's experimental kites, part of his research into flight and flying machines, pictured in a magazine in about 1904.

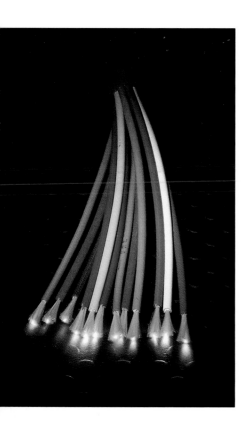

Light shining at the end of optical fibers. Bell's idea of "talking with light" has come about, with the use of optical fibers for telephone cables.

Talk on the move — telephones are now installed in cars, planes, trains, and even people's pockets. They work by radio signals and can even be used when walking along.

Chapter Seven
After Bell

The basic telephone that you hold in your hand and the way it works has changed little since the time of Bell and Edison. But there have been many amazing improvements in switching and dialing systems, and in telephone exchanges and networks. Most main phone lines today use light rather than electricity, just as Bell suggested. The signals consist of patterns of laser light shining along **optical fibers**.

In a telephone, sound patterns of speech are changed into signals of electricity or light. Other kinds of information besides speech can be converted into such signals, to be sent along the line. So phone lines convey computer information and coded images such as television pictures or documents and pictures from a fax machine.

Radio Links

Guglielmo Marconi invented radio 20 years after Bell invented the telephone. The two technologies of **telephony** and radio have come together in the modern, pocket-sized, go-anywhere mobile phone. Telephone networks also use radio and similar **microwave** links, instead of wires and cables, to carry their signals up and down to **satellites** in space or across large expanses of land or sea.

Achieving a Dream

A new development in telecommunications is the videophone, where you can see as well as talk to your caller. But the telephone still has a place in the lives and hearts of billions of people. It is a fitting tribute to a principle that Alexander Graham Bell cared about all his life — the importance of communicating with the human voice.

The newest great communications revolution is the videophone, where you see as well as hear the caller. But many people prefer to hide behind the traditional sound-only telephone.

The Bel

Alexander Graham Bell's name lives on today in the world of scientific measurements. The unit for the intensity of sound (loudness or volume) is called the bel. For normal use this is divided into 10, as decibels, dB. A whisper is 20-30 dB, normal conversation 60 dB, and loud music 90 dB.

In his Honor

The Alexander Graham Bell Institute for the Deaf is based in Washington, D.C. It is a world center for information on hearing difficulties and the problems they bring.

In the Name

Some inventions change name as they develop. Bell's device was known from the very beginning by the same name. The word "telephone" comes from two Greek words meaning far or distant and sound.

The World in Bell's Time

	1825-1850	*1851-1875*
Science	**1825** George Stephenson's *Locomotive No. 1* begins the first regular railway service **1847** Alexander Graham Bell is born in Scotland	**1859** Gaston Plante invents the rechargeable battery **1861** The telegraph line connects New York and San Francisco for the first time **1861** Physicist James Maxwell makes the first color photograph
Exploration	**1831** James Ross discovers the magnetic North Pole **1837** Beer and Madler make the first accurate map of the moon **1847** The first reports of gorillas reach Europe from Africa	**1853** The first railway lines and telegraph cables are laid in India **1859** Ferdinand de Lesseps starts work on the Suez Canal. It takes 10 years to build
Politics	**1833** British parliament abolishes slavery **1848** Karl Marx and Friedrich Engels write *Communist Manifesto*	**1861** American Civil War begins **1871** Rome becomes the capital of the newly united Italy
Art	**1843** The tuba becomes a regular member of the orchestra **1844-5** Alexandre Dumas finishes writing *The Three Musketeers* and *The Count of Monte Cristo*	**1858** Jacques Offenbach writes his operetta *Orpheus in the Underworld* **1860s** Claude Monet begins to produce his most famous works, known as impressionist paintings **1875** Mark Twain publishes *Tom Sawyer*

1876-1900	1901-1925
1879 Joseph Swan in England and Thomas Edison in the United States separately invent the first light bulbs	**1901** The first Nobel Prize for Physics is awarded to Wilhelm Roentgen, for the discovery of X rays
1888 Nikola Tesla invents the induction electric motor	**1903** Wilbur and Orville Wright make the first heavier-than-air powered flight
1888 Heinrich Hertz is the first to make and detect "Hertzian waves," later called radio waves	**1922** Alexander Graham Bell dies in Nova Scotia
1888 Fridtjof Nansen and his team complete the first land crossing of Greenland	**1904** Work begins on the Panama Canal
1891 Construction of the Trans-Siberian railway begins	**1911** Roald Amundsen is the first person to reach the South Pole
	1919 John Alcock and Arthur Brown make the first non-stop flight across the Atlantic Ocean
1877 In Japan, the Satsuma Rebellion ends the ancient tradition of Samurai power	**1908** Manchu power in China ends, soon followed by revolution
1891 In Britain, the Factory Act forbids children under age 11 to work in factories	**1914** World War I begins
	1917 Russian Revolution begins
1900 The Labor Party is founded in Britain	
1877 First performance of the ballet *Swan Lake* by Peter Tchaikovsky	**1904** Russian playwright Anton Chekhov finishes writing *The Cherry Orchard*
1883 London's Royal College of Music is founded	**1910** Kandinsky and Mondrian produce the first abstract paintings
1894 Richard Strauss composes his first opera, *Guntram*	**1911** The tango, a dance from Argentina, becomes the rage in U.S. and Europe

Glossary

acoustic: related to sound or the sense of sound. This word comes from the Greek *akoustiko*, from *akouein:* to hear.

battery: see *cell*.

campaign: to speak or demonstrate publicly in order to achieve an aim.

cell: in electrical work, a device containing various chemicals that produces a flow of electricity. More accurately, a single device like this is called a cell, and two or more linked together make a battery.

demonstration: a display or explanation showing how something works or a display or show protesting against something.

electric current: a flow of electricity through a substance, for example, through a metal wire.

facsimile: an exact copy or reproduction.

frequency: the number of times a vibration repeats itself in a certain time, usually one second.

laboratory: a building or room equipped for carrying out scientific research or for teaching practical science.

larynx: a muscular organ forming part of the air passage to the lungs. In humans it is in the neck and contains the vocal cords, and is called the voice box.

legal action: using the laws and rules of the country to show that someone has done something illegal (against the law).

magnetic field: an area or field of a magnetic force, in which a magnet exerts its *magnetism*.

magnetism: a still-mysterious force, produced by a magnet or an *electric current*, which can attract, repel, or change substances at a distance.

membrane: a flexible, sheetlike part. Membranes cover, line, or connect plant and animal organs or cells. They also form coverings or linings in machines.

microphone: a device used in sound systems for converting sound into electricity. The vibrations hit the diaphragm in the microphone and are converted into the equivalent patterns of electric current.

microwave: electromagnetic radiation, similar to light or X-rays, but in the *wavelength* range 0.3 to 0.001 meters.

network: a system of interconnected parts.

novelty: something that is unusual and interesting, but not necessarily useful.

optical fiber: a communications cable consisting of a thin glass fiber in a protective covering. Coded light signals transmitted along the fiber can contain sight, sound, or other information.

parchment: the skin of certain animals, such as sheep, treated to form a long-lasting material, as for bookbinding.

phonograph: an early form of gramophone capable of recording and playing back sound on wax cylinders, and later on plastic discs.

physiology: the branch of science concerned with the function of living things, that is, how they work. Vocal physiology is about the function of the voice.

power station: an electrical generating station.

rumor: information, often a mixture of truth and untruth, passed around usually by word of mouth.

satellite: an object orbiting the Earth or other object in space. Man-made satellites are used for communication, and transmitting or detecting information.

scarlet fever: a very contagious (catching) disease which gives people a fever, a strawberry-colored tongue, and a rash all over the body.

telegraph: a device or process by which information can be transmitted over a distance, especially using coded electrical signals. These are sent along a wire from a transmitter to a receiver, often in the dot-dash form of Morse code.

telephony: a system of communications for transmitting speech or other sounds.

trophy: a prize or object, such as a silver or gold cup, that symbolizes a victory in a contest or competition.

jB
BELL

Parker, Steve

Alexander Graham Bell
and the telephone

$15.95

DATE			

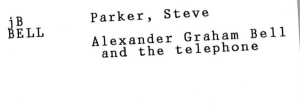